LANGUAGE

Lesley Newson

Contents

A&C BLACK · LONDON

The real problem with language

Do you have a problem with language? Do you sometimes forget how to spell or punctuate? Do you become tongue-tied at the very moment you want to say something? Are you struggling to learn a foreign language? This book isn't about any of those problems. It's about a problem that has been puzzling scientists and philosophers for centuries. And it probably puzzled people for thousands of years before anyone decided to call him or herself a scientist or a philosopher.

The mystery of language is: what is it and how did it come about? Why do we have the words we use? Who made up these sounds and gave them their meaning? How is it that every normal baby manages to work out how to understand and talk to the people around her? Is language special to humans or do animals have their own language that we don't understand?

One of the first things we learn is that humans are animals and yet we can't help feeling that we are quite different from other animals. The fact that we can talk is probably the main thing that sets us apart.

Children learn their first language in stages: understanding, talking, reading, writing. Learning a second language is usually more difficult.

From Martians at Mudpuddle Farm *by Michael Morpurgo,*
illustrated by Shoo Rayner

Authors of animal stories for children often make their animal characters talk, or show what the animals are thinking in words. We find it interesting to pretend that animals can talk and understand one another as we do.

Our ability to use language makes it possible to work together, to plan and do things that would be impossible for other animals. We can have arguments, reach agreements and explain our feelings. We can send information and ideas all over the world and leave a record of our thoughts for people who will be alive long after we are dead.

Does having a language also make us think in a way that is impossible for animals? We often think by talking to ourselves. Imagine trying to think things over if you didn't have words. Talking to yourself and others helps you to know who you are.

Puzzling out the mystery of language could give us a better understanding of what it means to be human. Today's scientists believe they may have found solutions to part of that puzzle. In early times, there were far fewer clues to go on but people still tried to work out answers to the mystery.

This is a scene from the Royal Shakespeare Company's production of King Lear, *by William Shakespeare. Shakespeare died nearly four centuries ago, but his words are still alive, allowing us to share the feelings of his characters.*

Early ideas

Many of our ancestors were not so much puzzled about why people can speak as about why different nations speak in different languages. They believed humans had been created to be able to talk just as dogs had been created to be able to bark.

But why didn't people all speak the same language? When explorers or merchants travelled to different lands, they found that the dogs barked in the same way as dogs at home, but the people seemed to talk gibberish. They understood one another but made no sense to the visitor.

The European Union is made up of many nations and many languages. The European Parliament in Strasbourg employs a staff of translators so that all the members of parliament can understand each other.

The Tower of Babel

A story in the Bible gives one answer to the mystery of why people speak different languages. According to the story, everyone spoke the same language until a ruler called Nimrod ordered his people to build a city with a tower so high that it would reach into the heavens. God didn't approve of this and put a stop to the building work by making the people of the city begin to speak different languages.

The city came to be called Babel or Babylon, which means 'confusion' and the tower was called the Tower of Babel. The people of the city could no longer work together or understand the orders of their rulers. Instead, they joined up with people who spoke the same language as themselves and travelled far and wide, setting up their own towns and villages.

Right: A Medieval painting of the Tower of Babel

A legendary experiment

Pharaoh Psamtik I ruled Egypt about 2700 years ago. According to legends, he carried out an experiment to discover which language had been the first to be spoken by all humans. He decreed that two infants be taken from their parents and not be allowed to hear anyone speak. Psamtik believed that, if the babies were never allowed to learn any other language, they might begin to speak to one another in that first language.

The babies were raised in a remote part of Egypt by a shepherd who couldn't speak. According to Psamtik, the first sensible word the children said was 'bekos'. This is the word for bread in the ancient language of Phrygian, which was once spoken in eastern Turkey. Psamtik therefore concluded that Phrygian must have been the original language.

No one knows if Psamtik really attempted to discover the original language to be spoken on Earth, but today's language scientists are sure that the experiment described in the legends couldn't have worked. Children learn to speak a language only if they hear other people speaking it.

From Babel to English

There are now about 5000 different languages spoken by the peoples of the Earth but why there are so many languages is no longer a mystery. Language is always changing. Old languages die and new ones are born. No one speaks Phrygian or the language of the Pharaohs any longer and when the story of the Tower of Babel was first told, the English language didn't exist.

About 1300 years ago, people in England were speaking a language called 'Old English'. The hymn pictured below, written in about AD 670, will give you an idea how different the language was in those days. Here are the first two lines with their modern English translation:

Nu   sculon herigean heofonrices
Now we must praise   heaven-kingdom's

Weard   Meotodes   meahte and his modgepanc.
Guardian the Creator's might   and his   mind plans.

It looks like a foreign language, but when you say the words out loud, some do begin to sound more like modern English; 'meahte' and 'might' for example, and 'heofon' and 'heaven'.

The first two lines of Geoffrey Chaucer's *Canterbury Tales*, written 600 years ago, show that the language of the people of England was gradually becoming much more like the language we speak:

Whan that April with his showres soote
the droughte of March hath perced to the roote . . .

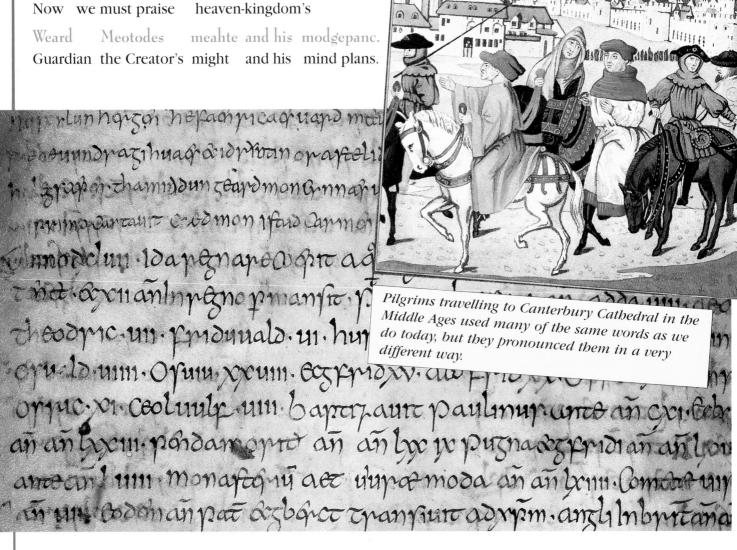

Pilgrims travelling to Canterbury Cathedral in the Middle Ages used many of the same words as we do today, but they pronounced them in a very different way.

◀ *The language spoken by people in old films isn't difficult to understand, but their accents may be slightly different from those usually heard today. Many new words have also been added to the English language during the last 50 years. What would people in those days have made of words like 'Internet' or 'digital stereo'?*

There are many examples of words that are different in British English and American English.

▼

New languages are born when groups of people start living apart and don't talk to each other any more. The language of each group changes in different ways until, after several hundred years of separation, the two groups find it difficult to understand each other.

When English-speaking people first moved to America, they spoke as they would have done in their home country: England, Scotland, Wales or Ireland. The language of the people on both sides of the Atlantic has changed and grown more different ever since.

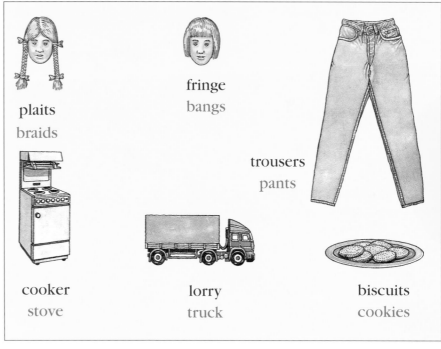

plaits
braids

fringe
bangs

trousers
pants

cooker
stove

lorry
truck

biscuits
cookies

It's not just the accent that is different; so are some of the words and the rules people follow as they speak. A teacher in the United States might say, 'You have only gotten a D on this assignment.' In England, the word 'gotten' isn't used anymore and 'assignment' is not a commonly used word. A teacher in England would be more likely to say, 'I was only able to give you a D for this piece of work.'

English-speaking people around the world sometimes have trouble understanding each other, but English probably won't divide to become new languages. Modern travel and communications mean that different groups of English-speaking people are never completely separate from one another. This was not the case in times past.

The people of Europe speak many different languages because, until quite recently, travel was dangerous. A stretch of water, a mountain range, even a thick forest was enough to separate communities. Soldiers and merchants did travel, but most people stayed at home, talked only to one another and thought that people in other places spoke strangely.

When famine or war meant that communities had to move or were invaded, the language was disturbed. Sometimes, the people would learn the language of the new region and their own language would die. More often, people merged their languages as they settled down together. You only have to look carefully at a language like English to see that this happens.

War and famine still create refugees. These people, fleeing Eritrea for Sudan, will also have the problem of adjusting to life in a new place where people speak differently.

Today's English is a mixture of words from many different sources. Words such as 'sheep', 'horse', 'dog', 'wood', 'field', 'work' and 'laughter', for example, are from Old English. They were brought to England in the 400s by Anglo-Saxon settlers who came from the countries we now call Denmark and Germany.

In the year 597 missionaries began to arrive from Rome and Ireland to teach Christianity to the English. They also taught them new words, such as 'angel', 'disciple', 'Sabbath', 'camel', 'lion', 'orange' and 'pepper', which came from Latin, Greek and Hebrew.

The Vikings invaded England several times between 750 and 1050. The language of the Viking settlers was similar to Old English and they soon learned the local language. The settlers kept some Viking words to use as well, though. Today, for example, you can 'wish' for something or you can 'want' it. 'Wish' comes from Old English and 'want' comes from the Old Norse language of the Vikings.

The Viking invaders from the countries we now call Norway, Sweden and Denmark may not have been welcome in England, but once they settled, their language merged easily with the language of the natives.

The Bayeux Tapestry is a pictoral record of the Norman Conquest of England which was created by 11th century needlework artists.

In 1066, William the Conqueror defeated the English King Harold at the Battle of Hastings. The new king spoke Norman French and expected everyone in England to learn his language. They didn't. A few hundred years later, even William's royal descendants were speaking English. However, by that time, Norman French words, such as 'peace', 'surrender', 'rule', 'royal', 'grand', 'pork' and 'beef', had been absorbed into the English language.

Looking closely at the derivation, or origin of words in our language can tell us why we speak the way we do, but it may also reveal clues to a much deeper mystery – how people began to speak in the first place. Archaeologists have dug up many examples of the tools and weapons our ancient ancestors invented, but surely their most important invention was language.

With so many different languages on Earth it could seem that language must have been invented many different times. But we know languages change, so it could be possible that all the Earth's 5000 languages have developed from just a few languages, or perhaps only one? The first clues to support this idea were discovered over 200 years ago.

Mother tongues

In 1783, an Englishman called Sir William Jones went to India to be a judge. Once there he decided to learn Sanskrit, the language of an important ancient Indian civilization. Sir William already knew two other ancient languages: Latin, which was spoken at the time of the Roman Empire, and the language spoken 3000 years ago by the people of the ancient Greek civilization. While Sir William was learning Sanskrit, he found that some words were strikingly similar to those in the other ancient languages.

Sir William was convinced this was not just a coincidence. The word for 'mother' is 'matar' in Sanskrit and 'mater' in Latin. 'Father' is 'pitar' in Sanskrit and 'pater' in Latin. Sir William found many other similiarities.

An intriguing similarity

Look at the numbers one to ten written in the three ancient languages:

	Latin	Greek	Sanskrit		Latin	Greek	Sanskrit
one	unus	heis	ekas	six	sex	heks	sat
two	duo	duo	dva	seven	septem	hepta	sapta
three	tres	treis	tryas	eight	octo	okto	asta
four	quattuor	tettares	catvaras	nine	novem	ennea	nava
five	quinque	pente	panca	ten	decem	deka	dasa

There are two possible reasons why languages have similar words. One is that the speakers of the languages picked up words from one another. But how could Sanskrit speakers of Ancient India have exchanged words with Latin and Greek speakers thousands of miles away on the northern shores of the Mediterranean?

The other reason seemed amazing but it was much more likely: the languages might have all developed from a single older language. It seemed reasonable that, long ago in prehistoric times, the ancestors of the people who spoke Latin and Greek both spoke the same language.

Sir William Jones's discoveries about Sanskrit suggest that even longer ago, there was a still more ancient language which had been spoken by the ancestors of Indians as well as Europeans. Just as these people were their ancestors, this language was the ancestor of a huge family of Indo-European languages. Language scholars have called this ancestor language 'Proto-Indo-European' ('Proto' is the Greek word for 'first').

Scholars learn ancient languages so they can read the documents, inscriptions and literature of ancient civilizations, such as the Ancient Greek inscription on this stone tablet.

Our language ancestor

Who were the people who spoke the first Indo-European language and why is their language the mother tongue of so many languages spoken today? An English archaeologist, Colin Renfrew, believes that they may have been a group of people who began to farm instead of hunting and gathering their food. He thinks they lived about 10,000 years ago on the fertile land between the Black Sea and the Mediterranean Sea.

As the children of these early farmers grew up, they moved out of this area to find new farmland. Over thousands of years, their farms spread across Europe and India. So did their language, but as the groups in different regions lost touch with their distant relatives, the single language became many.

Archaeologists have been able to trace the spread of farming from Turkey to Europe and India. Does this map also show the spread of our language ancestor?

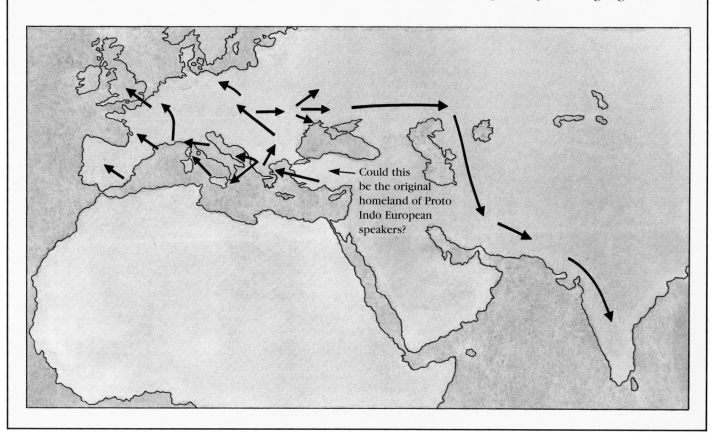

← Could this be the original homeland of Proto Indo European speakers?

If Proto-Indo-European was spoken 10,000 years ago, what languages were spoken by the people who lived even longer ago? The ancestor of the Indo-European language family must have had an even earlier ancestor. Many language scholars believe that all the world's 5000 languages may have descended from one great-great-grandmother tongue, the language spoken by the first people who talked.

As a result of Sir William's discoveries, language scholars began to think of a family tree of languages with new languages growing out like branches from older ones. They have been able to identify other language families. Arabic and many North African and Eastern Mediterranean languages belong to the 'Afro-Asiatic' family. Hungarian and Finnish, even though they are spoken in Europe, do not seem to be closely related to other European languages. Language scholars believe they are descended from an ancient language which they have called 'Uralic'.

When, how and why did humans start talking? One way to find clues is to compare ourselves with other animals.

Animal understanding

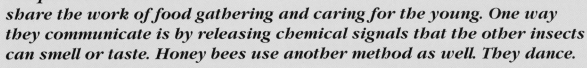

Other animals may not be able to talk, but they can tell each other things.

How bees communicate

Insects such as ants and bees have a complex communication system that allows thousands of them to live and work together. They build complicated homes and share the work of food gathering and caring for the young. One way they communicate is by releasing chemical signals that the other insects can smell or taste. Honey bees use another method as well. They dance.

A honey bee that has found a new place to gather nectar returns to the hive and begins to walk around in a figure eight. As she walks the middle of the eight, she shakes the back part of her body. The other worker bees watch her carefully and then fly directly to the place.

In 1945, the German biologist Karl von Frisch worked out the meaning of the dance. The walk in the middle part of the eight is the key. The direction of that walk tells the other bees in which direction to fly from the hive. If the walk is quite long, the other bees know to fly quite far. If it is short, they know the food is nearby.

Signalling underwater

Squid, octopus and cuttlefish send signals with their whole body. These animals can change colour, but unlike chameleons, they don't just use this as a way to camouflage themselves. A cuttlefish male who wants to mate with a female lets her know by making black and white zebra stripes run along his body. This also warns other cuttlefish males to stay away.

The animals we live with show us many examples of how they communicate: with smells and noises, body movement and shape. Some forms of animal communication are difficult for humans to understand. (What do dogs learn from sniffing each other's bottoms?) Others are much easier and even make it possible to communicate with our pets. We can teach a dog to understand when we want it to sit. Dogs can teach us to understand when they want to go for a walk.

A dog can only perform well when there is a good understanding between the dog and its trainer.

Animals can be surprisingly quick to learn signals. A cat can hear the sound of a tin opening from the opposite end of the house and be standing beside its bowl before you have begun to spoon out the food.

Do any animals have a way of communicating that is anything like human language? However good animals are at signalling to one another, it's plain to see that they can't say the same sorts of things as we do with our language. What is different about the way that humans communicate with each other?

This cat is using its body to send a signal. Humans also send messages by their gestures and postures. This is sometimes called 'body language', but does it compare to our spoken language?

Words

Animals that are closely related to humans, such as chimps and gorillas, make facial signals which are very similar to ours.

Humans can communicate with each other in many of the same ways that other animals do. We send silent signals to each other all the time. A smile can be a sign that a person is happy. We also make sounds that are similar to animal sounds. We cry, scream, even growl sometimes. The sound of a human voice gives the feeling behind the words and you don't have to be a human to understand. A pet dog knows it's being told off by the tone of its owner's voice.

But on top of all this, humans have language, our unique way of communicating. We use words. A word is a sound that means something. It doesn't have to be a sound, though. It can be a group of letters on a page. It can be hand movement that is part of a sign language. It can be a picture on a road sign.

You know perhaps 50,000 or more words and you can use them to say an almost endless number of things. That's because you know how to string words together to form sentences. You understand that words do different jobs in a sentence and you know exactly how to get them to work together for you.

When you say the word 'umbrella' a picture of an umbrella pops into the mind of someone listening to you. 'Umbrella' is a 'naming word' or *noun*. You use words that do different jobs to say things about the umbrella. Words called *verbs* say what the umbrella is doing and *adverbs* say how it is doing it. You can use *adjectives* to describe the umbrella.

You can put words together in a way that make sense, even if the sentence you make is silly.

The   angry   young   umbrella   ran   along   the   fallen   tree.
        adjectives   *noun*   *verb*   *adverb*   *adjective*   *noun*

If you said to your mother, 'The angry young umbrella ran along the fallen tree,' she would have a picture in her mind of an umbrella sprinting along a tree trunk. She might say you are talking nonsense, but it isn't nonsense. The sentence makes sense because the words are in the right order. The same words in a different order: 'young along the ran tree umbrella fallen angry the,' would be nonsense.

Words allow you to talk about almost anything. If you can talk to yourself, or think about something, you can talk to others and make them think about it too. If the words in a sentence are in the wrong order, they don't make sense. You know how to correct the sentence so that it does make sense.

You know that by changing a few words, you can change the meaning. You can ask why the umbrella ran along the tree. You can predict that it will run or say that it would have run if it hadn't broken its leg.

If you spoke Russian, German or Spanish you could say exactly the same things. You would simply use different words. The grammar you would use, the rules for how to organize the words, would be slightly different too, but if you had grown up with those languages, you would have learned how to organize them in a way that other people who spoke the same language would understand.

What is it that makes humans able to do this?

Humans don't need to hear or say words to communicate with a language. People who are fluent in sign language can express themselves as well as people using a spoken language.

The human sound machine

To say your 50,000 different words, you have to be able to make a variety of noises. In your throat, folds of tissue stretch like a pair of lips across the top of your windpipe. These are your vocal cords. When you are breathing they are spread wide apart and the air from your lungs rushes silently past them. They stay apart for some speech sounds such as 'sh', 'h' and 'f', but for most speech sounds they come together and vibrate. The vibration is your 'voice'.

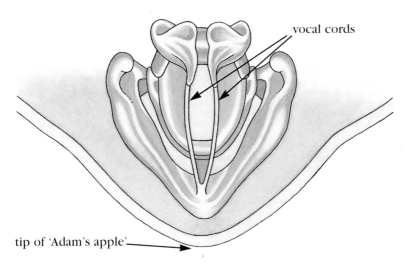

vocal cords

tip of 'Adam's apple'

That is just the beginning of the story though. On their own, your vocal cords can do little more that make a sort of humming noise. By using your mouth, nose, tongue, lips and teeth you can turn that hum into words. Try reading this sentence aloud slowly to yourself, thinking about what you're doing to make each sound in each word. To make different vowels sounds like 'e', 'a' and 'o', you are changing the shape of your mouth. To make the consonant sounds like 't', 'b', 'th' and 's' you are changing the position of your tongue and lips.

Children have to learn to make the sounds of their language. Speech therapists can help children speak more clearly and fluently by practising with them the sounds they find difficult.

The risks of talking

The ability to speak is worth a lot to humans and we pay quite a high price for it. The human throat and mouth are uniquely suited to making speech sounds. Other animals can't even begin to make the sorts of sounds that humans do. But the things that make your throat and mouth good at speaking, make them less good in other ways.

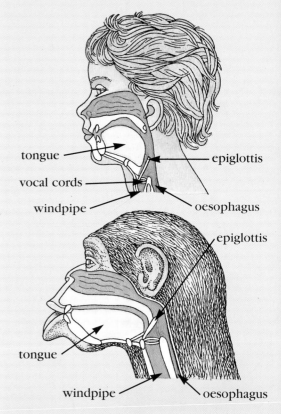

tongue
vocal cords
windpipe
epiglottis
oesophagus

epiglottis
tongue
windpipe
oesophagus

Humans, unlike other animals, have to live with the risk of choking. A chimpanzee is safe from choking because when it breathes, the opening at the back of its mouth seals shut and prevents food from going down the wrong way. The differences in the human throat that make speech possible also make it possible for food to slide down and block the windpipe.

To make its speech sounds, the human mouth has had to become shorter and rounder than a chimpanzee's, but humans and chimps have the same number of teeth in their jaws. Many people simply don't have enough room in their mouths for 32 teeth. Their over crowded teeth grow crooked or their wisdom teeth become impacted.

Wearing braces and having over-crowded teeth removed is the price some of us pay for having the human mouth's shape and the ability to make the sounds of speech.

We may be able to say 50,000 words, but have you noticed that groups of words which sound the same can often have quite different meanings? For example:

The stuff he knows could lead to problems.

The stuffy nose could lead to problems.

We rely on our brains to work out what the series of sounds mean. The human brain is very good at this and many poems and jokes that play with words exercise the brain's ability to make sense of words. Do you know this one?

I scream. You scream.
We all scream for ice cream.

Our brain's ability to understand words is even more amazing than our ability to speak them. When you first hear a foreign language, it can sound like a stream of gibberish. But when you know a language, your brain is somehow able to pick out each word. It can do this even if the words are whispered, distorted by a bad telephone line or spoken by someone with a strong foreign accent. The human brain is so good at sorting out the sounds of words, that we can talk quickly, run words together and miss out sounds.

People can manage to have a conversation even in a crowded room full of different voices saying different things.

Signs, tokens and chimps

The shape of a chimpanzee's mouth may make it impossible for it to talk, but chimpanzees are so very similar to us in other ways. Would it be possible to teach them to communicate with us?

Washoe makes the sign for 'hat'.

Teaching word signs

In the 1960s, Allen Gardner and his wife Beatrix began teaching a young female chimp called Washoe to use the sign language that deaf people in America use to talk to one another. Washoe lived in a caravan behind the Gardners' home in Nevada. The Gardners and some of their students had learned how to talk in signs. One or more of them were with Washoe all the time, talking to her and to each other, but only in American Sign Language.

Other chimps have also been taught to use American Sign Language. In this photo, three year old Tata is making the sign for 'drink' to Moja, aged six.

They hoped that Washoe would pick up the signed words in the same way that young children pick up spoken words by listening to adults. She did. In the first 21 months she learned 34 signs including 'come', 'gimme', 'hurry', 'sweet' and 'tickle' and as time passed she learned over a hundred signs. She also started putting signs together, saying things such as 'gimme tickle' or, when she wanted the refrigerator to be opened, 'open food drink'.

When Washoe was five years old, she went to live in a chimp colony at the University of Oklahoma. After her own baby died, Washoe was given a young male chimp called Loulis to adopt. In this experiment, people stopped signing to Washoe, to see if she would pass her language on to baby Loulis. She soon started trying to talk in sign language to him. During the next five years, Loulis learned over 50 signs from his signing mother.

Talking with tokens

At about the same time, a similar experiment was being carried out by a team of scientists led by David Premack at the University of California. They began teaching a chimp named Sarah to communicate by sticking plastic tokens onto a magnetic board. Each token was a word and Sarah managed to learn over a hundred words. Here are some of Sarah's words:

NOUNS

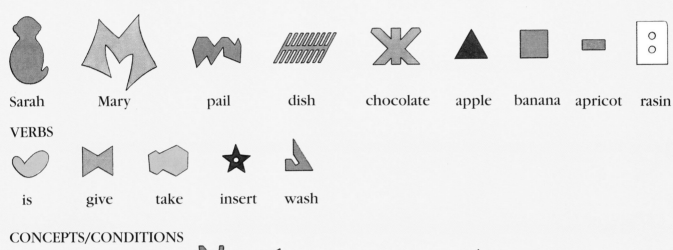

Sarah   Mary   pail   dish   chocolate   apple   banana   apricot   rasin

VERBS

is   give   take   insert   wash

CONCEPTS/CONDITIONS

same   different   no-not   name of   colour of   ?   if-then

ADJECTIVES (COLOURS)

red   yellow   brown   green

The scientists could use the tokens to give Sarah instructions like 'Sarah insert apple bucket.' Sarah learned to understand these instructions. When she did as she was told, she got a reward, usually a piece of chocolate. Sarah could also use the tokens to talk to her trainers. She would say things like, 'Mary give apple Sarah.' Once, Sarah put down the tokens to say 'give apple Gussie,' so her trainer gave the apple to Gussie, another chimpanzee who lived near Sarah. Sarah never made that mistake again.

Since the 1960s, experiments with chimpanzees have shown that they can be taught to learn 'words' and put them together to say things. But there is a huge difference between the language ability of apes and humans. Chimpanzees have been known to learn over a hundred words. By the time a human child is four, it has a vocabulary of over 1500 words.

Learning to talk

It seems remarkable that chimps can be taught to talk. But, when you think about it, isn't it much more remarkable that you learned your 50,000 words? You didn't have a team of experts to teach you. You were just surrounded by a chattering family. It was no one else's job to teach you words. People just spoke to you when they felt like it and told you 'no' if you did something wrong. When you began to talk, everyone was delighted but no one was surprised. It's happened billions of times before. It's what babies do.

In the 1950s an American language scientist called Noam Chomsky began to point out how very surprising it is that babies learn to talk. He also suggested that there might be something special about the way we learn language. We don't seem to learn it in the way we learn to read or do arithmetic. It almost seems as though the brains of babies are programmed to learn to talk.

Noam Chomsky changed psychologists' ideas about the way children learn language.

John Oates of the Open University is finding out which sounds and pictures are most interesting to this baby.

Detecting a baby's feelings

How do the psychologists that study babies know when a baby is interested? It isn't as difficult as it might seem. All babies like to suck and some like to suck on a dummy. Psychologists have noticed that when a baby is interested in something, it sucks more quickly than when it is bored. So to find out how interested a baby is, they give it a dummy connected to a machine that calculates how rapidly the baby is sucking.

Using this method, psychologists have found that babies find the sound of the human voice much more interesting than any other noise.

Tuning in to language

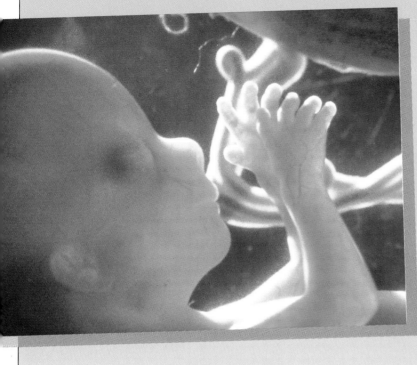

In 1988, psychologists Jacques Mehler and Peter Jusczyk played recordings of people speaking French and Russian to four-day old French babies. The babies were most interested in the sound of French. Russian was not so interesting to them and later experiments showed that they were just as bored with English and Italian.

How could four-day-old babies know that French is their language? The psychologists believe it is because they had been listening to that language while they were inside their mothers' wombs. The mothers all spoke French and the babies had already tuned in to the sound of the language.

Chomsky and other scientists have made many detailed studies of babies learning to talk and these have supported the idea that humans are born with the special ability to learn language. For one thing, the sound of the human voice is much more interesting to babies than any other noise.

Another thing that makes scientists believe babies are programmed to learn language is that all normal babies go through the same stages as they learn to talk. Between the ages of five and seven months, they start making noises that sound like voiced speech sounds. By eight months they are practising word sounds like ba-ba-ba, neh-neh-neh, and dee-dee-dee. Once children reach their first birthday, they are babbling out a long stream of sounds that seem to be consonants and vowels. It can sound just like speech but it's complete gibberish.

Babies who are born deaf learn sign language in the same way as other babies learn to speak. At the same age that hearing babies begin to talk gibberish, deaf babies start babbling too, with their hands. If a baby is born without the ability to hear, it is important that this is detected as early as possible. Then people will know that they must 'speak' to the baby in other ways. This will allow the the baby to learn to talk in sign language.

Are the brains of parents also programmed to teach their babies to talk?

Just before their first birthday, babies start to understand words and, shortly after that, most begin to say them. For a while, they just say one word at a time. Then they start putting them together to say things like 'daddy do', 'see cat' or 'shoe off'. Babies all over the world say the same sorts of thing when they speak their first tiny sentences. In different languages words are often said in a different order. Babies almost always manage to use the word order that is correct for the language they are learning.

Parents are often amazed at how quickly their toddler picks up new words.

Average size of vocabulary (number of words)

After a while, the sentences grow to be three or four words long and then, between the age of about three and three and a half, children seem suddenly to be able to talk quite freely. They begin to put the little words like 'the', 'in', 'to' and 'has' into their sentences. This lets them say very complicated things like: 'I want to stand in the shower so Daddy won't find me'.

Children do make mistakes with their grammar. They may sometimes say 'I are' instead of 'I am' at first, but they actually make far fewer mistakes than adults learning a foreign language. Tiny children who can't put together the simplest jigsaw can put together the words to say things most older people couldn't say in a second language even if they had studied it for months.

Between the ages of one-and-a-half and six-and -a-half, children's vocabulary increases rapidly.

English-speaking three year olds work out that people say 'that cow' if there is one cow and 'those cows' if there is more than one. As if by magic, they know that this works for lots of things. They say 'that tractor' and 'those hens'. No one is surprised when they make the mistake of saying 'sheeps' and 'calfs' but it doesn't take long for them to work out that they should be saying 'those sheep and calves'. At the same time, they are learning lots of other rules of grammar. They learn to put '-ed' on the end of a word like 'walk' if they walked in the past but not to say 'goed', 'sitted' and 'thinked'.

Scientists have found that all children of this age suddenly pick up speech in this way whatever language they're learning. We seem to lose this ability as we become adults. This is why many people find learning a language very difficult when they are older.

A young child might say: 'Me feed sheep', but she soon learns to say: 'I'm feeding the sheep'.

Young children are most interested in talking and listening to adults. As they grow older, they learn to have fun with people of their own age.

Some parents believe they must correct their children's mistakes to help them learn to speak. However, scientists have compared families which try to teach their children to talk with those who don't. The studies found that all the children progressed at more or less the same rate. To learn to talk, it seems that human babies just need people to listen to and people to talk to.

Even more remarkably, children seem to be able to find a way to talk to their friends, even if they don't speak the same language.

How children beat Babel

Imagine living in a crowded village made up of people who spoke several different languages. This was the life of millions of children who grew up between the years 1500 and 1900, whose parents had been captured or bought and forced to work as slaves or labourers on plantations. The adults had to work long hours growing sugar, fruit, tea or other plantation crops. The children were just left to play together.

The plantation bosses didn't bother to learn the languages of their workers. They just ordered them about saying things like: 'You, go there,' or 'Look him. Do that.' The workers soon learned enough words to understand the orders.

The children learned the language of their parents, but often their friends spoke a different language. The children could talk together in the simple sort of language used by the bosses, but found it frustrating because it didn't have the word changes and little words that make it possible for people to say what they really mean. In other words, the bosses' language didn't have rules of grammar like a proper language.

The children soon found a way to talk, though. They spoke a new language, based on the language of the bosses, but with its own grammar that the children made up. This seems to show that children aren't just programmed to learn grammar. They can invent it, too.

The people who traded, transported and used slaves seemed to block from their minds that they were fellow human beings.

Inventors of grammar?

In the 1970s, an American language scientist called Derek Bickerton began studying the speech of people who had learned to speak on an Hawaiian plantation. One 92 year old man said to him: 'Me cap buy, me check make'. He meant to say: 'He bought my coffee. He made me out a cheque', but he couldn't really make his meaning clear. Bickerton found that this man had been brought to Hawaii as an adult, so he had only learned the simple language of the bosses.

When Bickerton spoke to younger people who had grown up on the plantation, he found that they didn't speak in the same way at all. For example, one woman said: 'Bin get one wahine she get three daughter'. In English this translates as: 'There was a woman who had three daughters'. She is speaking what scientists call a 'creole' language. It's made up mostly of English words, which the plantation workers had learned from the bosses, but unlike the bosses' language, it has a grammar which allows the people who speak this language to put together the words to say exactly what they want. Bickerton realised that this grammar must have been invented by the children of the plantation.

Workers harvesting sugar cane on an Hawaiian plantation in the 1930s.

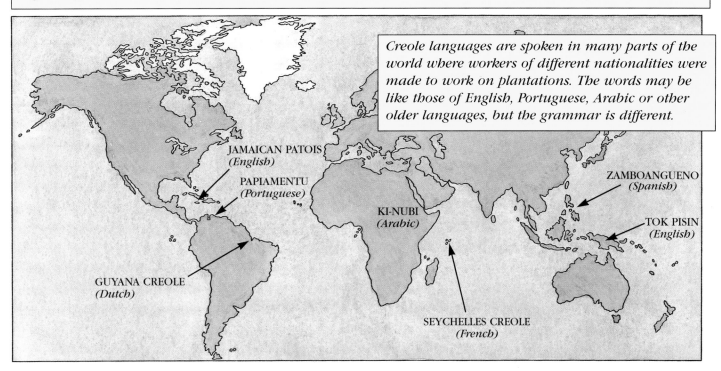

Creole languages are spoken in many parts of the world where workers of different nationalities were made to work on plantations. The words may be like those of English, Portuguese, Arabic or other older languages, but the grammar is different.

JAMAICAN PATOIS
(English)

PAPIAMENTU
(Portuguese)

GUYANA CREOLE
(Dutch)

KI-NUBI
(Arabic)

SEYCHELLES CREOLE
(French)

ZAMBOANGUENO
(Spanish)

TOK PISIN
(English)

This brain is made for talking

If humans are programmed to learn language, the program must be stored in the human brain. The brain learns words and how to say them. It sends signals to the muscles of the mouth and throat to make them produce just the right sounds. Just as your throat is much better at making speech noises than a chimpanzee's, your brain is better at making language.

The brains of humans and chimpanzees look similar but the human brain is bigger and a slightly different shape.

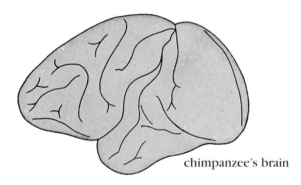

chimpanzee's brain

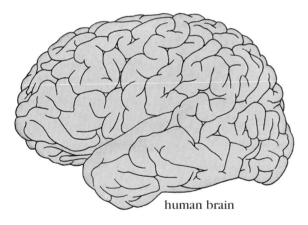

human brain

One way scientists learn about the brain is by studying people who have suffered brain damage. A stroke often causes damage to only a small part of the brain and the sort of harm it does is linked to the area where the damage is.

Discovering the brain's speech areas

Many people who have had strokes find speaking difficult. In the 1860s a French scientist called Paul Broca showed that a certain type of speech problem called aphasia is almost always linked to damage in one area on the left hand side of the brain. People with damage in Broca's area speak slowly and without grammar.

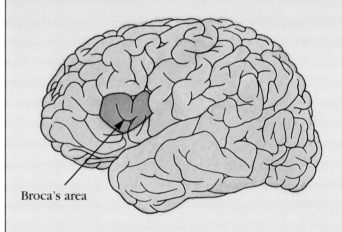

Broca's area

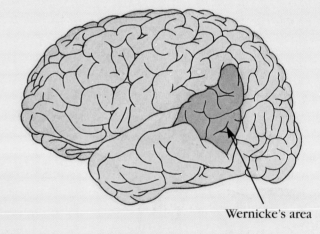

Wernicke's area

One patient talking about a dental appointment said: 'Yes . . . Monday . . . Dad and Dick . . . Wednesday nine o'clock . . . 10 o'clock . . . doctors . . . and . . . teeth'. When patients try to write, they make the same errors. Yet patients with this kind of damage can still sing, draw and copy writing from a book. Their problem is only in thinking out how to say things. Perhaps Broca's area is where the human grammar program is stored.

Some people lose their ability to speak if part of their brain is damaged by a stroke. They may be able to talk again if another area of the brain develops to do the work of the damaged part. Learning to speak again is hard work for people who have had a stroke. They need help and encouragement from speech therapists and other and medical professionals.

Another of the brain's speech areas was discovered by the German scientist Carl Wernicke in 1874. It's also on the left hand side of the brain. People with damage in this area can say words in a pattern that is grammatically correct, but they use the wrong words or made-up words. When one patient with damage to this area was asked why he was in hospital, he said, 'Boy am I sweating, I'm awful nervous, you know, once in a while I get caught up, I can't mention the tarripoi, a month ago. . .'

From their study of stroke damage in patients, scientists now know that there are two areas of the brain, called Broca's area and Wernicke's area, which play a key role in speech. But damage to other brain areas can also change a patient's ability to speak. In a few cases, Wernicke's and Broca's areas have been undamaged but the nerves connecting them to the rest of the brain have been destroyed. Patients with this problem eerily repeat everything that is said to them but can't think of anything to say for themselves.

As scientists learn more about how the brain works, they may learn more about how it works to make us speak. Meanwhile, other scientists are trying to puzzle out how human beings developed a brain that was made for talking.

Family members can also help stroke victims learn to cope with their speech problems.

Working out a story of long ago

How did human beings become the only animal with a brain and a voice that allow it to talk? Scientists are trying to piece together ideas and clues about language to work out how humans began to talk. The people who told the Bible story of the Tower of Babel believed that God created all the living things on Earth just the way they are today and that God created humans with the ability to talk. But now we know that the mystery of language is much deeper than this.

We know that the Earth and its living things haven't always been as they are today. Evidence from fossils shows that many of the animals and plants that lived long ago were very different from those living today. Most scientists believe that living things change or 'evolve' over time and that these very different animals and plants are the ancestors of those living today. For most of the Earth's long history there were no humans. Most scientists believe that human beings and apes evolved from the same ancestors and that chimpanzees are our closest relatives.

So, sometime in the past, there lived an animal,which was the common ancestor of both chimps and humans. This animal probably couldn't talk any better than a chimp, but since then, the human side of the family evolved a throat that can make voice sounds and a brain that can learn and use language.

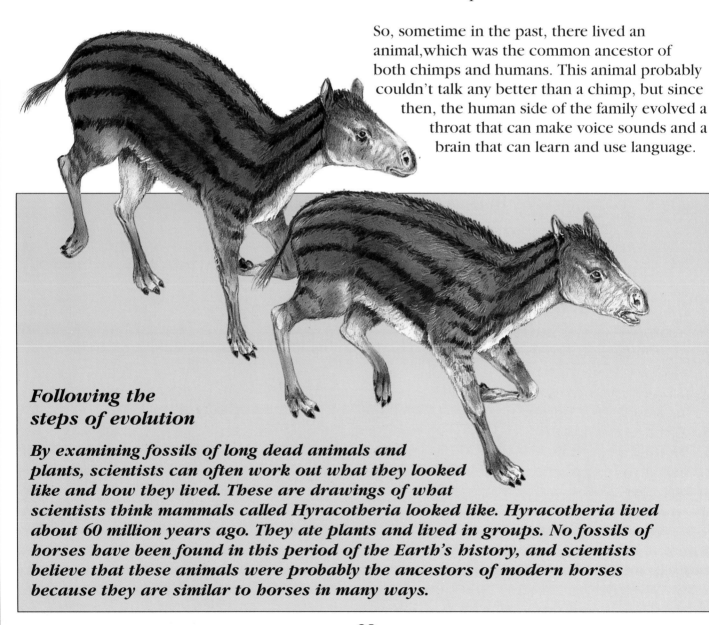

Following the steps of evolution

By examining fossils of long dead animals and plants, scientists can often work out what they looked like and how they lived. These are drawings of what scientists think mammals called Hyracotheria looked like. Hyracotheria lived about 60 million years ago. They ate plants and lived in groups. No fossils of horses have been found in this period of the Earth's history, and scientists believe that these animals were probably the ancestors of modern horses because they are similar to horses in many ways.

How and when did our ancestors evolve their ability to use language? A clue may lie in the split in the ape family tree between the non-talking chimp family and our own human family. Is there a way of working out when this split happened?

The body chemical DNA carries genetic information from parents to children and holds a kind of record of our evolution. By comparing the information on DNA samples from chimps and humans, scientists have found that the split between the chimp family and the human family happened about five million years ago. In other words, five million years ago an animal lived which is the ancestor of both chimpanzees and humans.

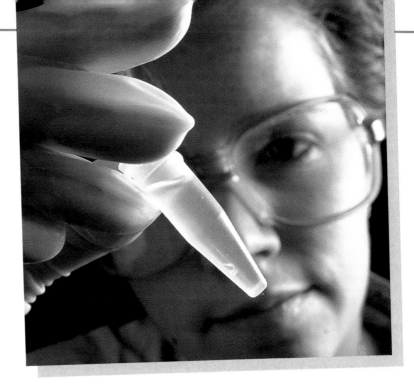

This is a sample of DNA, extracted from human cells.

Darwin's theory of evolution says that changes occur in living things by accident. Animals evolve because a few of these changes create an animal that has a better chance of surviving and producing young. The beneficial changes are passed on to the next generation.

Language is a system of communication completely different from that of any other animal. Some people find it hard to believe that such a complex ability could have evolved in only five million years. They suggest that some purpose drove this rapid development. Could a higher being have had a hand in our creation? It's impossible to test ideas like this scientifically, but it is possible to investigate the fossils of creatures who were probably our ancestors.

There are also many differences though, notably in their feet. Hyracotheria had toes like other mammals. Fossils of more recent horse-like animals show a series of changes in the feet. The more recent fossils have outer toes that are smaller and claws that are larger and more hoof-like. This record of fossils provides one of the clearest demonstrations of how an animal evolved. As if to provide further evidence, every so often a mare gives birth to a foal with one or two small toes beside its main hoof.

Charles Darwin's book The Origin of the Species *(1859) described his studies of plants and animals from around the world and explained why he believed they evolved by 'natural selection'.*

Fossils of early human-like creatures don't give a clear picture of how humans or our language evolved, but they have given scientists some clues.

The oldest human fossil found so far lived 100,000 years ago.

Australopithecus lived 3 million years ago

Homo habilis lived 2 million years ago

Homo erectus lived 750,000 years ago

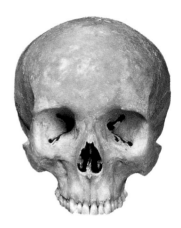

Homo sapiens sapiens (modern human)

An American scientist called Jeffrey Laitman has compared the fossil skulls pictured here, and believes he can tell the shape of the throat by looking at each skull. Laitman thinks that Australopithecus, the earliest of the human-like creatures had a throat like a chimpanzee, but that more recent skulls show the throat becoming more human in shape. These creatures may not have sounded just like us, but, Laitman thinks, they probably could have made sounds which allowed them talk to one another.

The shape of the insides of the fossil skulls can tell us something about the brain that once rested there. They show that, over time, the brain becomes more human in shape. In one Homo habilis skull, it's possible to see that the brain had a small bulge on the left hand side in the same position as 'Broca's area' in the modern human brain. The American scientist Ralph Halloway believes it shows that this ancestor already had a brain which was programmed to use language.

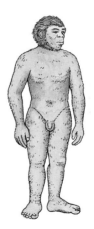

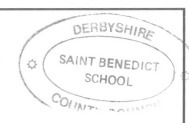

Five million years ago, ape-like creatures lived which were the ancestors of both chimps and humans. Today, the human side of the family has changed to develop a way of life completely different from that of any other animal. Each change that improved our ancestors' ability to talk, allowed them to get the upper hand on creatures who were less gifted in language. They could plan and co-operate with one another more easily and this made them better able to obtain food, build things, teach each other and look after their children.

Biologists have analysed the DNA in blood samples taken from people all over the world to find out how closely related people are. Their analysis shows that every human being on Earth shares a common ancestor who lived between 150,000 and 200,000 years ago. There were many other people living at that time, but the descendants of that person are the only people alive today. They took over the world and many scientists believe that they were able to do this by being better talkers than the other humans.

By looking at how closely related people are in different parts of the world, it's possible to track the movements of the human family and see when some members first left Africa and began their spread around the world.

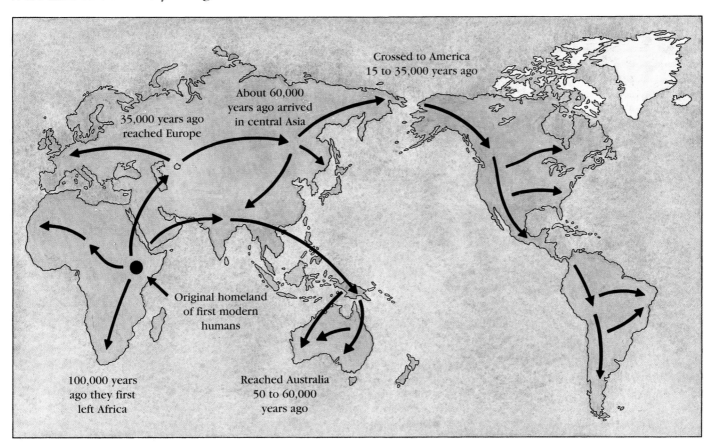

The work of the biologists in tracking the spread of the human family backs up the work of language scholars who have looked at the way different language families have spread. The people of nations whose languages are similar, whose languages belong to the same language family, are also most closely related genetically. The evidence from our languages and our DNA supports the idea that our branch of the human family arose in Africa and slowly colonized the rest of the world.

As our human family moved and separated, new languages were born and old ones died. Different sides of the family evolved to look slightly different. They sometimes fought and took over each other's land. But the evidence scientists have found shows that we are all one family, and in the beginning we probably all spoke one language. In some ways, the story the scientists tell isn't very different from the Bible story of the Tower of Babel and the beliefs of many religious thinkers and philosophers.

Acknowledgements

The author and publisher would like to thank the following for their help in the preparation of this book: Sara Bernard, Phase 0, Amsterdam Medical Centre; Don Mitchell, Washington Singer Laboratories, Department of Psychology, University of Exeter; John Oates, Centre for Human Development and Learning, School of Education, Open University; Stephen Pinker, Department of Brain and Cognitive Sciences, Massachusetts Institute of Technology; Colin Renfrew, McDonald Institute for Archaeological Research, Cambridge University; Karl Sabbagh, Skyscraper Productions; Edmund Weiner, Oxford English Dictionaries.

The illustration on pages 2/3 is taken from *Martians at Mulpuddle Farm* written by Michael Morpurgo and illustrated by Shoo Rayner.

Photographic credits
Front cover clockwise from bottom right: Royal Shakespeare Comapany/ Donald Cooper, Mary Evans Picture Library, Gerard Lacz/NHPA, C.M.Dixon; back cover (top) Syndics of Cambridge University Library, (bottom) Dr Maurice Cross

p2 (bottom) Chris Fairclough Colour Library; p3 (bottom) Royal Shakespeare Company/ Donald Cooper; p4 European Parliament; p5 Mary Evans Picture Library; p6 (left) Syndics of Cambridge University Library; (right) Mary Evans Picture Library; p9 Hulton Deutsch Collection Ltd; p8 (top) Maggie Murray/Format; (bottom) Laurie Campbell/NHPA; p9 Mary Evans Picture Library; p10 (top) Mary Evans Picture Library, (bottom) C.M. Dixon; p12 Stephen Dalton/NHPA; p13 (top) Dr Geoffrey W. Potts, (middle) Marc Henrie, (bottom) Jim Bain/ NHPA; p15 Sally and Richard Greenhill; p16 Hattie Young/Science Photo Library; p17 (top) Gerard Lacz/NHPA, (bottom left) Ulrike Preuss/Format, (bottom right) Hulton Deutsch Collection Ltd; p18 (both) B.T. Gardner, University of Nevada; p20 (top) Rex Features Ltd, (bottom) John Oates CHDL Open University; p21 (top) Petit Format/Nestle/ Science Photo Library, (bottom) Judy Harrison/Format; pp22-23 (all) Chris Fairclough Colour Library; p24 Mary Evans Picture Library; p25 Royal Geographical Society, London; p27 (top) Judy Harrison/Format, (bottom) Bubbles; p28 Natural History Museum Picture Library; p29 (top) Lesley Newson, (bottom) Mary Evans Picture Library; p31 James Holmes, Cellmark Diagnostics/Science Photo Libary; p30 Natural History Museum Picture Library.

First published 1996
A & C Black (Publishers) Limited
35 Bedford Row
London WC1R 4JH

ISBN 0-7136-4026-X

A & C Black (Publishers) Limited

A CIP catalogue record for this book is available from the British Library.

Illustrations by Jason Lewis

Index